CAPE VERDE
TRAVEL GUIDE

Must See And Do in Cape Verde, Where Thrills, Togetherness, And Romance Await

Amber Reed

Copyright © 2023, Amber Reed

No part of this publication may be reproduced, distributed, or transmitted in any form or by any means, including photocopying, recording , or other electronic or mechanical methods, without the prior written permission of the publisher, except in the case of brief quotations embodied in critical reviews and certain other

Table of content

MAP OF CAPE VERDE   **5**

  Map Of Praia   6

INTRODUCTION   **7**

OVERVIEW OF CAPE VERDE   **9**

  Geography and climate Cape Verde   12

  Brief history and culture Cape Verde   14

  Why Visit Cape Verde   17

  Entry requirements and visa   20

  Currency And Exchange Rates   22

GETTING TO CAPE VERDE   **25**

  Transportation Options   27

  Island Hopping Cape Verde   29

  Accommodation Options   32

TOP DESTINATIONS   **37**

  Praia   37

  Mindelo   39

  Sal   42

  Boa Vista   45

  Santiago   48

ACTIVITIES AND ATTRACTIONS   **51**

  Hiking And Nature Trails   51

  Cultural festivals and events   54

  Shopping and souvenirs   56

  Local cuisine and dining options   60

  Water Sports   63

  Couples Activities   66

  Family Friendly activities   71

Cape Verde Travel Guide

Off-the-beaten-path destinations 74

Practical Information **77**

Health And Safety Tips 77

Language And Communication 80

Useful phrase 83

Local customs and etiquette 85

FAREWELL **89**

MAP OF CAPE VERDE

Map Of Praia

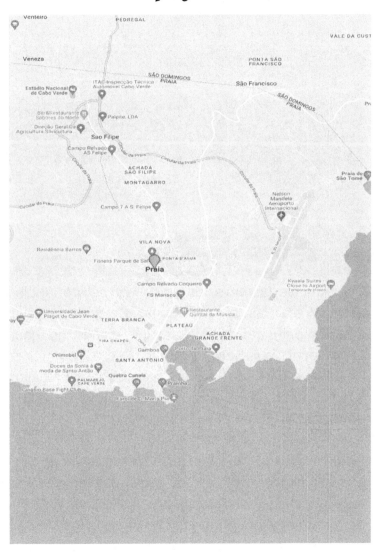

INTRODUCTION

The Atlantic Ocean's turquoise waves are lapping at your feet as a warm wind whispers through swaying palm palms. You're engrossed in the tunes of a local musician, relishing each mouthful of freshly caught fish. This is Cape Verde, a location where reality and paradise meld into a perfect dance.

I can promise you that Cape Verde is more than just a place to visit; as an avid traveller who has explored these islands, it's an awakening. With the help of this guide, I hope to show you Cape Verde's true nature rather than simply another destination to cross off your list. We'll see the must-see locations, partake in the must-do activities, and become fully immersed in the colorful fabric of Cape Verdean culture.

However, this is a promise rather than merely a travel guide. a pledge of priceless experiences, deepening relationships, and comprehensive knowledge of this special region of the globe. This guide is your pass to an incredible journey, regardless of your interests-be they beachcombing, culture-seeking, or daring exploration.

Why then should you believe this guide? It's a compilation of my most treasured memories and local insights, thus it's a labor of love. It's the outcome of many hours spent discovering undiscovered coves, chatting with locals, and falling in love with Cape Verdean friendliness.

Are you prepared to go on a journey that will both satisfy your need for travel and warm your soul? As we travel across the remarkable landscapes, customs, and flavors of Cape Verde, let this book serve as your compass. It is an honor to be your guide on your journey across Cape Verde.

OVERVIEW OF CAPE VERDE

Cape Verde, officially the Republic of Cabo Verde, is an island republic in the Atlantic Ocean off the northwest coast of Africa. With ten major islands and several smaller islets, Cape Verde is renowned for its breathtaking scenery, rich cultural diversity, and distinctive fusion of European and African influences.

Located about 350 miles (570 km) off the coast of West Africa, in the Atlantic Ocean, is the volcanic island archipelago known as Cape Verde. The nation is split between two groups of islands: the Leeward Islands (Sotavento) in the south and the Windward Islands (Barlavento) in the north. The islands range in size from large and rugged to small and deserted. They have a great variety of environments, from verdant valleys to arid deserts.

Cape Verde's capital and largest city, Praia, is situated on the island of Santiago. The people of Cape Verde are varied, with influences from both Europe and Africa. Although Cape Verdean Creole, or Kriolu, is commonly spoken, Portuguese is the official language.

The history of Cape Verde begins in the fifteenth century, when Portuguese explorers arrived and found the island uninhabited. After that, Portugal colonized it. During the transatlantic slave trade, the islands were a major stopover for ships bringing Africans slaves to America. After gaining independence from Portugal in 1975, Cape Verde instituted a democratic political system.

The culture of Cape Verde is a blend of Portuguese, African, and other European elements. The music, dancing, and food of the nation all reflect this. A fundamental part of Cape Verdean culture are musical genres like funaná and morna. Performers such as Cesária Évora have received praise from all around the world for their work.

The main sectors of Cape Verde's economy now include banking, tourism, and remittances, having formerly relied heavily on agriculture. The nation has grown in popularity as a travel destination. The economy also heavily depends on agriculture and fishing, especially on islands with richer soil.

The gorgeous seas, immaculate beaches, and abundant marine life of Cape Verde are well-known. Hiking, water activities, and cultural experiences are the main draws for tourists visiting the islands. São Vicente, Santiago, Boa Vista, and Sal are among the well-liked tourist spots.

With multi-party political parties, Cape Verde is a democratic republic. As the head of state and government, the President does double duty.

Cape Verde is renowned for its kind people, varied culture, and stunning natural surroundings. Cape Verde provides a distinctive and warm experience in the Atlantic Ocean, whether you're looking for outdoor activities, cultural discovery, or just some downtime on sandy beaches.

Cape Verde Travel Guide

Geography and climate Cape Verde

Geographically, Cape Verde is composed of ten larger islands as well as a number of smaller ones. The Leeward Islands (Sotavento) in the south and the Windward Islands (Barlavento) in the north are the two groupings of islands. Santiago, the largest and most populated island, is home to the capital city of Praia. Some more well-known islands include Boa Vista, Sal, Santo Antão, and São Vicente.

The varied topography of the islands consists of mountains created by volcanic eruptions as well as level, sandy plains. Some islands have desert landscapes, while others have breathtaking mountain peaks. The highest peak in Cape Verde is the Pico do Fogo in Fogo Island, which is approximately 2,829 metres (9, 281 feet) above sea level. On the island, there is also an active volcano.

The subtropical desert environment of Cape Verde experiences a noticeable dry season. The charming temperatures and sparse precipitation of the islands set them apart. November through July typically marks the beginning of the dry season, whereas August through October marks the beginning of the wet season. Throughout the rainy season, Cape Verde may have periodic storms and heavy rainfall.

The weather in Cape Verde is mild and pleasant throughout the year. September and October are the hottest months, with daily highs of 25°C to 30°C (77°F to 86°F). Even during the warmest months, the coastal communities benefit from the moderate ocean breezes.

There is some precipitation, especially during the dry season. Variable islands get varying quantities of precipitation; some are quite dry, while others receive more. The rainy season brings the majority of the year's precipitation, which generally takes the form of heavy but brief downpours.

The northeast trade winds have a significant influence on the islands during the dry season. These breezes maintain a pleasant and moderate weather.

Although they don't often strike Cape Verde, hurricanes can nevertheless occur there at any time of the year. However, the archipelago is outside of the typical storm patterns.

Cape Verde Travel Guide

Cape Verde's unique geography provides a variety of scenery, ranging from breathtaking beaches to volcanic peaks.Tourists seeking outdoor adventures and relaxation find it a year round destination due to its stunning landscape and amiable, temperate climate. Travelers of all kind may find something to enjoy in Cape Verde, whether they wish to explore the coast, hike the mountains, or just relax on the sandy beaches.

Brief history and culture Cape Verde

With a rich history and a dynamic culture that combines elements of African, European, and other influences, Cape Verde officially known as the Republic of Cabo Verde has plenty to offer. The islands of Cape Verde were deserted before Portuguese explorers arrived. In the fifteenth century, the Portuguese made the discovery of the archipelago.

After being colonized by the Portuguese, Cape Verde was an important part of the Portuguese Empire. For Portuguese ships traveling to Africa, the Americas, and Asia, it was an essential port of call. As a major hub for the transatlantic slave trade, Cape Verde was visited by a large number of Africans who were being sold into slavery and headed for the Americas. Slave trafficking operations exploited the islands as a centre.

An independent-minded nationalist movement gained traction in the middle of the 20th century. In 1975, Cape Verde broke away from Portuguese rule. Aristides Pereira served as the nation's first president.

The Modern Era Cape Verde has had political stability and economic growth since gaining its independence. From being mostly dependent on agriculture, its economy has expanded to include services, tourism, and remittances from the Cape Verdean diaspora.

African, Portuguese, and other European influences have blended to create the distinctive culture of Cape Verde. The food, dancing, and music of the nation all reflect this. With musical traditions that include morna, funaná, and coladeira, Cape Verde is well known for its music. The "Barefoot Diva, " Cesária Évora, was a great contributor to the global discovery of Cape Verdean music.

Live music frequently complements the colorful and passionate traditional Cape Verdean dance styles.

Cape Verde Travel Guide

Dance is an essential part of the nation's cultural fabric.

The fusion of civilizations may be seen in the food of Cape Verde. Usually, dishes combine elements of European and African cuisine. Grains, legumes, maize, and an assortment of meats and seafood are staples.The national food is regarded as "cachupa," a stew made with maize, beans and pork.

Cape Verde has a number of festivals and annual events. Especially on the island of São Vicente, carnival is a vibrant event that features colourful parades, music, and dancing.

Although Portuguese is the official language of Cape Verde, the local dialect, known as Kriolu, is widely spoken and varies depending on the island.

Handmade goods like ceramics, jewellery, paintings, and textiles are produced in Cape Verde's flourishing arts and crafts industry.

The history of Cape Verde is characterized by a stormy colonial past, a resilient heritage, and the ultimate quest for freedom and nationhood. African and European influences have interacted to create a rich and colorful tapestry of music, dance, and food in its culture. In addition to experiencing this distinctive fusion of customs, visitors to Cape Verde may take in the friendliness and kindness of the local populace.

Why Visit Cape Verde

Known as "the African Caribbean," Cape Verde is a lure with a distinct appeal and a plethora of attractions that make it a perfect trip. Explore this island nation for the following convincing reasons.

- ❖ Some of the most beautiful and pristine beaches in the world may be found in Cape Verde. The turquoise seas and white dunes are ideal for swimming, lounging, and water sports. Beautiful beaches may be found on islands like Sal and Boa Vista.

- ❖ Arid deserts, verdant valleys, and volcanic vistas are all part of the country's varied topography. For those who enjoy the outdoors and hiking, Cape Verde is a fantastic vacation because of its variety.

- ❖ African, Portuguese, and other European influences have blended to create the distinctive culture of Cape Verde. The islands' dancing, music, and gastronomy all reflect their rich cultural past.

- ❖ With genres including morna, funaná, and coladeira, the Cape Verdean music culture is well-known across the world. These contagious musical genres frequently have upbeat dancing forms that are accompanied by their rhythms.

- ❖ Numerous museums and historical places offer an exploration of the history and impact of this era, which was crucial to the transatlantic slave trade and which included Cape Verde.

- ❖ Cape Verde is a haven for lovers of water activities, with steady trade winds. Popular sports include deep-sea fishing, windsurfing, kitesurfing, and surfing.

- ❖ Awe-inspiring scenery can be seen across the islands, including the Paul Valley, the stunning Tarrafal Beach, and the Pico do Fogo volcano.

- ❖ People from Cape Verde are renowned for their friendliness and kindness. You'll discover a friendly environment with a sincere desire to share their culture with guests.

- ❖ African and European influences may be found in the blend of flavors and ingredients found in Cape Verdean cuisine. Eat some of the regional specialties, such as "pastéis" and "cachupa. "

- ❖ Ecotourism and environmental preservation are priorities for Cape Verde. Sustainability and protecting the islands' natural beauty are major themes in many lodgings and activities.

- ❖ With their own personalities and allures, Cape Verde's islands provide a chance to discover a range of experiences. Cape Verde is an ideal getaway from the winter blues because of its warm and sunny environment, which makes it a year-round resort.

Because of its stunning natural surroundings, diverse culture, and friendly people, Cape Verde is a great place to visit for anybody looking for an exceptional and unforgettable trip in the Atlantic Ocean. Every type of traveler may find something to enjoy in Cape Verde, whether they are seeking adventure in varied landscapes or beach leisure.

Entry requirements and visa

Most travelers to Cape Verde require a visa to enter the country. Visa exemptions may apply to citizens of certain countries, including some African, European, and South American nations. The duration of visa free stays can vary. Typically allows a stay of up to 90 days for tourism and recreational purposes.

Issued for business-related travel, including meetings, conferences, and negotiations.

Student Visa, For individuals who plan to study in Cape Verde. Required for individuals who intend to work in Cape Verde. Visa applications are typically submitted to a Cape Verdean embassy or consulate in your home country.

You'll need to provide a completed visa application form, a valid passport with at least six months of validity beyond your intended departure date, a passport-sized photo, and proof of accommodation. Additional documentation may be required depending on the type of visa you are applying for. Visa processing times can vary, so it's advisable to apply well in advance of your intended travel date.

Cape Verde also offers a "visa on arrival" option for some nationalities. This allows travelers to obtain a visa at the airport upon arrival. However, not all countries are eligible for this option, so it's essential to check whether it applies to your nationality and the specific conditions that may apply.

Ensure your passport has at least six months of validity beyond your intended departure date from Cape Verde.

Please note that entry requirements, visa regulations, and visa fees can change, so it's crucial to verify the latest information with the nearest Cape Verdean embassy or consulate or through official government channels. Additionally, travelers are encouraged to have travel insurance that covers any unexpected events during their trip.

Currency And Exchange Rates

The official currency of Cape Verde is called the Cape Verdean Escudo (CVE). It can be represented by the symbols "$" or "Esc. " The Bank of Cape Verde issues and oversees the currency.

Exchange Rates: Before transferring money or making any financial transactions, it is advised to confirm the current rates since they are subject to change.

Currency exchange services are available in major international airports, banks, exchange offices, and certain hotels in Cape Verde.

Although the Cape Verdean Escudo is the official currency, several establishments catering to tourists may also take payments in euros (EUR) or US dollars (USD). Nonetheless, it is more typical to do transactions in local money.

ATM: There are several ATMs across Cape Verde from which you may withdraw either Cape Verdean Escudos (CVE) or, in some situations, US dollars. Using an ATM to get local money when visiting is frequently useful.

Credit Cards: Major credit cards, such Visa and MasterCard, are accepted at most tourist destinations and bigger businesses. Still, it's a good idea to carry extra cash in case of little transactions or at locations that might not take credit or debit cards.

Visitor's Checks: In Cape Verde, traveler's checks are typically not accepted. For your financial transactions, it's best to use cash, credit cards, or ATMs.

Before transferring money, it is crucial to confirm the current currency rates because they are subject to change. Also, keep in mind that there can be costs involved in foreign ATM withdrawals and currency exchange. When traveling to Cape Verde, it might be helpful to have a combination of major foreign currency and Cape Verdean Escudos to facilitate financial transactions.

GETTING TO CAPE VERDE

The majority of visitors fly internationally to get to Cape Verde. There are four international airports in the country: Cesária Évora Airport on São Vicente Island, Nelson Mandela International Airport on Santiago Island, Amílcar Cabral International Airport on Sal Island, and Aristides Pereira International Airport on Boa Vista Island. Numerous international airports serve these flying destinations.

Flights to Cape Verde: There are flights to Cape Verde from a number of European and African locations operated by major international airlines, such as TAP Air Portugal, TUI Airways, and Cabo Verde Airlines (previously TACV). Travelers from Europe may easily reach Cape Verde because direct flights from that continent are frequent.

Cruise: Cruise ships are making more and more stops in Cape Verde, especially during the winter. Cape Verde is occasionally a stop on European cruises, particularly those that originate in the Canary Islands. An other method of seeing several islands in one trip is via cruise.

Cape Verde Travel Guide

Visa Requirements: Make sure you have obtained the required visa in advance of your trip to Cape Verde. While some nations may be eligible for visa waivers or visas on arrival, most visitors must have a valid passport in order to enter the country. Examine the visa requirements specific to your country of residence and your itinerary.

Travel Documents: Verify that your passport will be valid for at least six months after the date you want to depart Cape Verde.

Local transit: Once in Cape Verde, you may travel between the islands using local transit, such as domestic aircraft and taxis.

Before you book your trip, make sure you are aware of the most recent travel warnings, visa requirements, and entry restrictions for Cape Verde. Think about the particular island or islands you want to visit as well, as each has its own special attractions and experiences. Depending on your place of departure, Cape Verde is a reasonably accessible location with a range of aircraft options.

Transportation Options

To assist you in seeing the islands, Cape Verde provides a range of transportation choices. The most popular means of transit in Cape Verde are listed below, however they may differ depending on the island:

Domestic Flights: The main islands may be reached by domestic aircraft. Cabo Verde Airlines and Binter CV are two Cape Verdean airlines that run these services.The busiest airports, with links to neighbouring islands, are found on Santiago Island and Sal Island. Longer distances between the islands can be easily traveled by air.

Taxis: Taxis are a typical way of transportation on the majority of islands. They're easily found in airports and cities. Before you leave, bargain with the driver about the fare. For shorter excursions inside towns, shared taxis, or "aluguers, " are more popular and cost-effective. They frequently pick up many people and travel predetermined itineraries.

Car Rentals: Many of the islands provide car rentals, giving visitors freedom and flexibility while they explore. Major airports and bigger towns are home to rental businesses. Remember that on certain islands, the roads might range from smooth to rough, so pick a car that will fit the desired itinerary.

Local Buses: Santiago and São Vicente in particular have public bus service on their islands. Although their timetables might not always be dependable, they are a reasonably priced mode of transportation. The largest public bus system is found on Santiago Island.

Walking and Hiking: Walking is a practical method to explore because many cities and tourist destinations are pedestrian-friendly. Particularly on the more hilly islands like Santo Antão and Fogo, Cape Verde provides an abundance of paths for hiking and trekking enthusiasts.

Ferries and Boats: Ferries and boats are utilised to go between islands and are a necessary part of inter-island transportation. There are local ferries that may be used for shorter excursions between nearby islands.

Marine taxis, or taxis marítimos: Sal and Boa Vista are two islands that provide water taxis. Transfers from the airport to hotels around the coast frequently take place using these.

Rental Bicycles: You may rent bicycles in some tourist locations to explore the region. Especially on flat, less populated islands, this is a terrific way to explore at your speed.

ATVs and Dune Buggies: For off-road exploration, you may rent ATVs or dune buggies in locations like Sal and Boa Vista.

Equestrian Touring: You may tour certain islands, like Santo Antão, on horseback, offering a distinctive viewpoint of the topography.

Keep in mind that there can be differences in the accessibility of some services and the availability of transit choices across smaller or less developed islands. When visiting Cape Verde, it's a good idea to arrange your transportation according to the islands you want to visit and the kinds of activities you want to do.

Island Hopping Cape Verde

Island hopping is an excellent method to see the unique natural beauty and rich cultural heritage of the Cape Verdean archipelago. You may explore the finest of Cape Verde via island hopping, since the country is home to 10 main islands and numerous smaller islets, each with its own distinct experiences. Some advice for island hopping in Cape Verde is provided below:

Cape Verde is separated into two groups: the north's Windward Islands (Barlavento) and the south's Leeward Islands (Sotavento). Every group has unique qualities. Based on your interests, choose which islands you wish to visit. For instance, Santo Antão provides breathtaking hiking options, and Sal and Boa Vista are renowned for their lovely beaches.

Make a pre-planned itinerary for your island hopping. Flights connecting Cape Verde's islands are well-connected, especially between Sal, Boa Vista, Santiago, and São Vicente. It is advisable to verify the airline schedules and reserve your tickets in advance, particularly during the busiest travel seasons.

Because of Cape Verde's year-round mild temperature, island hopping is feasible throughout the year. But you really need to think about the weather and the things you want to do.

Reserve your lodging in advance on each island. There are several hotels and resorts in well-known tourist locations like Sal and Boa Vista, although there are fewer housing alternatives on some smaller islands.

Be ready to travel between islands and explore using a variety of local transport options, including domestic planes, ferries, and local buses.

There are several activities available on every island. Whether it's hiking, water activities, or cultural immersion, make time to discover the distinctive features and adventures that every island has to offer.

The stunning beaches of Sal and Boa Vista, the hiking paths atop Santo Antão, the São Vicente music scene, and Santiago's ancient charm are just a few of the island's features.

On every island, indulge in regional Cape Verdean cuisine. Every region has its unique specialty in food, like the well-known cachupa.

Accept the distinctive music, customs, and culture of each island. Attend and take part in local celebrations and activities when they happen.

Remember to bring your camera to document Cape Verde's breathtaking scenery and dynamic culture.

You may explore the archipelago's diversity by island hopping in Cape Verde, from sandy beaches and arid landscapes to lush highlands and energetic city life. A memorable voyage full of one-of-a-kind experiences and magnificent vistas may be created with careful planning and an adventurous attitude.

Accommodation Options

To accommodate a range of spending limits and tastes, Cape Verde has a selection of lodging choices. A wide range of accommodations are available, including boutique hotels, guesthouses, and luxury resorts. An outline of the many lodging options in Cape Verde is provided below:

Hotels and Resorts: There are several hotels and resorts in Cape Verde, the majority of them are located on the well-known islands of Sal and Boa Vista. These places have a variety of amenities, such as dining options, drinking areas, water sports centres, and swimming pools High-end amenities and stunning beachfront sites are two of the luxury resorts' most well-known features.

Cape Verde Travel Guide

Bed & Breakfasts and Guesthouses: A more personal and deeply immersed experience may be had on a number of islands by staying at guesthouses or bed & breakfasts. Families from Cape Verde frequently own and run them. These alternatives may be more affordable and offer the chance to interact with people and take in genuine Cape Verdean culture.

Vacation Rentals: There are a number of islands where you may find vacation rentals, such as flats, villas, and holiday houses. For people who would rather have a private space where they can cook and unwind, they're a fantastic alternative. Vacation properties in Cape Verde are often listed on websites such as Booking. com and Airbnb.

Hostels: Offering both private and dormitory-style rooms at more reasonable prices, hostels are an inexpensive vacation choice, especially on islands like Santo Antão and Santiago that are popular with backpackers.

Eco-Lodges: Located on islands such as Santo Antão and Fogo, eco-lodges emphasise eco-friendly and sustainable tourism. They frequently provide hiking and outdoor activities.

Boutique and Small Hotels: There are boutique and small hotels on several islands, such as São Vicente and Santiago, which provide a more individualized and distinctive experience.

Camping: While it's not as popular as other lodging options, camping is still possible in some locations if you want a more daring stay.

Luxury Villas: On several islands, like Sal and Boa Vista, luxury villas and private apartments are offered to those looking for an upscale experience.

While selecting your hostel, keep in mind that accommodations may differ from island to island depending on the specific places you intend to visit.

To ensure the finest selection, it's a good idea to reserve your lodging in advance, particularly during popular tourist seasons. Cape Verde provides a variety of lodging options to ensure a comfortable and memorable stay, regardless of your travel goals-leisure, adventure, or cultural immersion.

TOP DESTINATIONS

Praia

Situated on Santiago Island, Cape Verde's capital and largest city is called Praia. It serves as the nation's hub for politics, the economy, and culture.

In addition to housing the National Assembly and the presidential mansion, Praia is the capital city of Cape Verde. The settlement is located with a view of the Atlantic Ocean on Santiago Island's southern shore. It features a charming waterfront and lovely beaches.

Kebra Kanela Beach and Quebra Canela Beach are two of Praia's many lovely beaches. These locations are well-liked for water sports, swimming, and sunbathing.

Praia's historic district, the Plateau, (Platô) is home to vibrant buildings from the colonial era, quaint streets, and colonial-era architecture. Numerous stores, eateries, and marketplaces in the city are located here. Numerous music festivals, art exhibitions, and cultural events take place in the city all year long, contributing to its thriving cultural environment. Here, morna is a very popular traditional music genre.

Explore the local markets in Praia, such Sucupira Market, where you can buy fresh vegetables, handmade crafts, and other items.

Cidade Velha, or Old Town, is a UNESCO World Heritage Site and a short drive from Praia. Known for its colonial-era architecture and historic attractions, it was the first European colony in the tropics.

Other noteworthy sites in Praia are the Diogo Gomes Square, which bears the name of the

Portuguese explorer who found Cape Verde, the Presidential Palace, and the Praia Cathedral.

You may enjoy outdoor activities in and around Praia, including hiking, discovering Santiago Island's untamed landscapes, and participating in water sports along the shore.

Praia provides stunning seaside scenery, a combination of history, and culture. The city is vibrant, combining contemporary conveniences with traditional Cape Verdean culture. Praia is a must-visit location for anybody visiting Cape Verde, whether their interests lie in discovering the city's historic core, unwinding on its beaches, or indulging in the local food and music.

Mindelo

Located on São Vicente Island, Mindelo is the second biggest city in Cape Verde. It is renowned for its busy nightlife and music scene, gorgeous shoreline, and thriving cultural environment.

Many people refer to Mindelo as Cape Verde's cultural centre. The vibrant music culture in the city is well-known, and it is the birthplace of famed Cape Verdean singer Cesária Évora, popularly known as the "Barefoot Diva." The city holds a number of music festivals and annual cultural events.

Cape Verdean music, which includes funaná, coladeira, and morna, is centred on Mindelo. Local taverns and clubs have live music performances that are enjoyable for visitors. One of the highlights of the Cape Verdean music calendar is the city's renowned Baía das Gatas Music Festival.

The colonial-era architecture, vibrant buildings, and cobblestone streets of the city's historic centre are well-known features. It's a fun place to stroll about.

The lively Mercado do Peixe (fish market) and Mercado Municipal (municipal market) are great places to buy fresh seafood, produce, fruits, and handicrafts made in the area.

The city's waterfront neighbourhood is charming and dotted with eateries, bars, and cafés. You may unwind there, take in the views of the ocean, and watch the boats sail by.

Laginha Beach and São Pedro Beach are well-liked locations for swimming and sunbathing. Along the shore, there are many other water activities to attempt.

Consider visiting Monte Verde, the island's highest point, for expansive views of São Vicente and Mindelo. You may take a taxi or walk to the top of the mountain.

Savor the fresh fish, rice, beans, and regional stews that characterise Cape Verdean cuisine in Mindelo. International and traditional foods are served at restaurants.

Cesária Évora International Airport (VXE), the airport serving Mindelo, provides access to a number of other Cape Verdean islands.

Mindelo has one of the most vibrant carnival celebrations in Cape Verde, attracting attendees from all around the archipelago and beyond. It's a terrific spot to buy unique gifts since you may visit the local artisan stores and art galleries.

The warm environment, musical traditions, and rich cultural legacy of Mindelo make it a lively and intriguing place to visit. Mindelo is a popular Cape Verdean destination whether you're a music fan, an art enthusiast, or just looking for a vibrant and diverse ambiance.

Sal

Sal, renowned for its breathtaking beaches, water sports, and lively resort districts, is one of the most visited tourist sites in Cape Verde. Some of Cape Verde's most exquisite beaches may be found near Sal. With its lengthy lengths of white sand and turquoise waves, Santa Maria Beach is the most well-known. Swimming, tanning, and water activities are all quite welcome here.

For lovers of water activities, the island is a dream come true. You may go deep-sea fishing, snorkelling, scuba diving, windsurfing, and kitesurfing.

Salinas de Pedra de Lume: Situated in the caldera of an extinct volcano, these salt pans are a singular natural attraction. The very salinity of the water is claimed to be comparable to the Dead Sea, allowing you to float freely in it.

Shark Bay: Known for its pristine, tranquil waters, Shark Bay, also known as Baía das Gatas, is a great place to swim and snorkel. Lemon sharks are friendly to people, and you may even see them in the bay.

The Kite Beach: The steady breezes at Kite Beach make it a popular site for kite surfers. In addition, you may unwind on the sandy beaches while taking in the activity.

Town of Santa Maria: This is the island's primary tourism centre, including a range of lodging options, dining options, entertainment venues, and retail stores. Particularly in the nights, it's a bustling and energetic spot.

Regional Dining: Visit the island's eateries to experience the native cuisine, which features fresh seafood. The national meal, cachupa, grilled fish, and lobster are a few of the delicacies of the area.

Scuba Diving and Snorkelling: Sal has fantastic snorkelling and diving conditions. Discover vibrant aquatic life, underground caverns, and shipwrecks.

Sal International Airport: The primary point of entry for foreign visitors to Cape Verde is the Amílcar Cabral International Airport (SID) located on Sal. There are frequent flights from this well-connected airport to a number of foreign locations.

Beachside Bars and Entertainment: Sal has a thriving nightlife culture that includes clubs and beachside pubs with live music, dancing, and a welcoming vibe.

Relaxation: Sal is a terrific spot to relax and take in the laid-back Cape Verdean way of life, even though it's well-known for its water sports and exciting entertainment.

For those who enjoy the beach and water activities, Sal is a great location. It's the ideal location to take in the sun, thrilling outdoor pursuits, and the culture of the Cape Verdeans. Sal offers activities for all types of people, whether they are looking for adventure or leisure.

Boa Vista

One of the most popular islands in Cape Verde, Boa Vista (meaning "Good View" in Portuguese) is renowned for its immaculate beaches, sand dunes, and striking natural settings.

Praia de Santa Mónica: one of Cape Verde's longest beaches with kilometres of golden sand, is one of the most beautiful beaches in Boa Vista. Beautiful beaches with options for swimming, water sports, and sunbathing include Praia de Chaves and Praia de Curralinho.

Sand Dunes: Much of the island is covered in sand dunes in the northeastern Viana Desert, which is sometimes compared to the Sahara Desert. Hiking, sandboarding, or just relaxing and soaking in the amazing views are all made possible by the dunes, which create a distinctive and scenic scenery.

Marine Life: Submerged Life The abundant marine life of Boa Vista is well-known. Particularly Loggerhead sea turtles may be seen breeding on the beaches here. On the island, there are initiatives to save turtles, and you could be lucky enough to see a hatch.

Sal Rei: The hub of activity on the island is Sal Rei, the principal town on Boa Vista. You may stroll around the town's busy marketplaces, eat fresh seafood at eateries, and take in the lively ambiance.

Water Sports: Strong, steady breezes make for great windsurfing and kitesurfing conditions at Boa Vista. Numerous water sport rental stores and schools exist.

Espingueira Shipwreck: On the island's western shore, have a look at the Espingueira shipwreck.

It's a strange and interesting sight that provides insight into the island's seafaring past.

Sal Rei Harbor: A great place to see the boats and take in the local atmosphere is the harbor. Restaurants and pubs with views of the waterfront are available.

Quad Biking and Off-Roading: Embark on an off-road or quad bike adventure to explore the interior of the island and find hidden treasures. This is a fantastic opportunity to see Boa Vista's lesser-known areas and desert vistas.

Local Cuisine: In Sal Rei and other nearby towns, savor the delectable Cape Verdean cuisine, which includes seafood and traditional specialties.

Whale Watching: Whale watching is a popular activity in Boa Vista. Booking boat cruises allows you to get up close and personal with these amazing creatures, which migrate across the waters around Cape Verde.

Boa Vista is a haven for anyone looking for quiet island living, outdoor activities, and unspoiled natural beauty. Boa Vista provides an unforgettable Cape Verdean experience, whether your interests lies in beachcombing, water sports, or just taking in the peace and quiet of unspoiled surroundings.

Santiago

Of the Cape Verdean islands, Santiago is the biggest and most populated. It is the centre of the nation's politics and culture and provides a wide variety of experiences.

Praia: Situated on Santiago Island, Praia serves as the capital city of Cape Verde. It serves as the country's hub for politics, the economy, and culture. Praia's bustling marketplaces, Praia Harbor, and the old Plateau neighbourhood are its highlights.

Cidade Velha: One of the earliest European colonies in the tropics, Cidade Velha is only a short drive from Praia. It is recognized as a UNESCO World Heritage Site. It is well-known for its colonial architecture, ancient sites, and breathtaking views of the shore.

Culture: Music festivals, art shows, and a bustling street life are all part of Santiago's vibrant cultural landscape. In the taverns and clubs in your area, you may listen to classic music genres like coladeira and morna.

Cape Verde Travel Guide

Sotavento Beaches: Tarrafal Beach, with its golden sands and crystal-clear waves, is one of the stunning beaches on Santiago's southern shore. Swimming and other water activities are prominent at Tarrafal.

Hiking and Trekking: Santiago has excellent hiking options and is renowned for its diverse scenery. Some of the places to walk include the Assomada Plateau, Serra da Malagueta, and Pico d'Antónia.

Regional Dinning: Savor the fresh fish, grilled meats, and traditional dishes like cachupa and catchupa that characterise Cape Verdean cuisine in Santiago. The best venues to try the island's delectable cuisine are the local markets.

Monuments and History: The São Filipe Fort, Pelourinho, and the Presidential Palace in Praia are just a few of the historical and cultural landmarks of Santiago.

Dance and Music: The music and dancing scenes of Santiago Island are very lively. At neighbourhood get-togethers and festivals, traditional music like funaná and batuque is frequently played.

Monte Tchota: Beautiful views of Santiago and the nearby islands may be seen by hiking up Monte Tchota. It's a fantastic way to discover the island's breathtaking scenery.

Handcrafted and Local Art: Visit the neighborhood's craft stores and art galleries to buy one-of-a-kind mementos and encourage local artists.

Santiago Island is a historical and cultural gem that combines urban and outdoor activities. Santiago offers a wide variety of things for visitors to explore and enjoy, from seeing the vibrant city of Praia to trekking in the picturesque interior of the island and taking in the native way of life.

ACTIVITIES AND ATTRACTIONS

Hiking And Nature Trails

Outdoor enthusiasts and those who like the great outdoors will find Cape Verde to be an excellent getaway due to its abundance of hiking and nature paths. There are many different environments to explore, ranging from lush highlands to dry deserts.

Santo Antão: also called the "Island of Mountains," provides some of Cape Verde's most breathtaking hiking experiences. Deep valleys, rough mountain terrain, and verdant surroundings may all be found on the island. Popular hiking spots in Santo Antão include the Paul Valley and the Cova Crater.

Serra da Malagueta Natural Park: located on Santiago Island, With hiking routes up to the peak of Serra da Malagueta, where you can take in expansive views of Santiago Island, this natural park is home to a variety of flora and animals.

Pico d'Antónia: hike to Pico d'Antónia, Santiago Island's highest peak, and enjoy the interior of the island's beautiful magnificence.

Cape Verde Travel Guide   51

Ribeira do Paúl (Santo Antão): Terraced fields, abundant greenery, and the charming settlement of Vila das Pombas are the valley's defining features. You may explore the agricultural traditions of Cape Verde by hiking in this area.

Fogo National Park: located on Fogo Island: One of the most famous hiking locations, the Pico do Fogo, is located in Fogo. You may hike to the peak of the volcano for a unique experience, and the crater offers a weird lunar view.

Ribeira Principal (São Nicolau): Ribeira Principal is one of the most picturesque hiking paths in São Nicolau. You'll have the chance to see the island's interior and breathtaking scenery as well as the customs of the locals.

Monte Gordo, São Nicolau: For amazing views of the surrounding countryside, hike to the peak of Monte Gordo, the highest point on São Nicolau.

Pedra Badejo Natural Park: located on Santiago Island, This seaside park is a great place for nature lovers and bird watchers since it has a variety of habitats and hiking routes.

Serra Malagueta: Discover the wooded areas and meandering paths of the Serra Malagueta range. Offering expansive vistas, the tallest mountain is known as Serra Malagueta.

Cruzinha da Garça (Santo Antão): Enjoy the rough nature of the island while strolling along this picturesque coastline walk on Santo Antão's north shore.

You may discover Cape Verde's varied terrain via hiking, which includes lush valleys, mountains, volcanic craters, and seaside paths. Prior to starting your hiking expeditions, be sure to examine the local environment and path availability. For a more engaging and secure experience, think about hiring a local guide.

Cape Verde Travel Guide

Cultural festivals and events

A nation rich in culture, Cape Verde has a long history of festivities, dance, and song. Visitors may immerse themselves in the local way of life and take in vibrant entertainment at a number of cultural festivals and events held throughout the year. The following are a few of the major cultural celebrations and occasions in Cape Verde:

Music Festival Baía das Gatas (Baía das Gatas, São Vicente Island): This is one of Cape Verde's most well-known music festivals, and it takes place every August. It attracts music lovers from all over the world with a varied roster of regional and international performers.

Theatre Festival Mindelact (São Vicente Island, Mindelo): An esteemed international theatre festival called Mindelact takes place in Mindelo every year. It offers a platform for regional and global talent by showcasing a diverse array of theatrical acts.

Music Festival Gamboa, in Praia, Santiago Island: Celebrated in the capital city of Praia, this music festival showcases worldwide music

Cape Verde Travel Guide 54

performers with a range of musical styles, such as the Cape Verdean morna, coladeira, and funaná.

Tabanka Festival (Santiago Island): May sees the annual Tabanka dance and music event on Santiago Island. It is influenced by African rhythms and Cape Verdean culture. Vibrant parades and energetic entertainment are features of the event.

Festival Internacional de Música da Gamboa (FIMG, Gamboa, Praia, Santiago Island): An eclectic range of musical genres may be heard at the international music festival FIMG. It draws artists from outside as well as those from the area, and it happens on Gamboa Beach.

Fiestas de São João (São João Festival, Santo Antão Island): One of the most vibrant celebrations on Santo Antão takes place in June. It features traditional music, dance, and colorful processions.

Carnival São Filipe (Fogo Island): Celebrated with colorful costumes, parades, and music, Fogo Island's Carnival of São Filipe is a spectacular festival.

Boa Vista Island's Praia D'Águada Festival: This local music festival at Praia d'Águada on Boa Vista is a terrific opportunity to get a taste of the local culture and highlights artists from Cape Verde.

Carnival: Across Cape Verde, funfair is observed with vibrant parades, dancing and music. Every island has distinctive Carnival customs and festivities of its own.

Sal Island's International Festival de Morna (FIM): The popular music genre in the nation, morna, is the focus of this event. It highlights the cultural significance of morna in Cape Verde and includes performances by well-known performers.

Discovering Cape Verdean music, dance, and customs is made possible by these cultural festivals and events. They provide guests with a distinctive and enjoyable experience as they frequently incorporate a blend of regional traditions and global influences.

Shopping and souvenirs

From vibrant markets to quaint boutiques and artisan stores, Cape Verde has a wide range of shopping options. There are many choices available, whether you're searching for traditional Cape Verdean goods, one-of-a-kind handcrafted things, or souvenirs. In Cape Verde, consider these options for shopping and mementos:

Handmade goods: Brightly colored baskets, woven items, and textiles are among the handicrafts that are well-known from Cape Verde. Local markets and craft stores carry these products. Seek out "panos" (fabrics) and "cestos" (baskets) featuring classic Cape Verdean patterns.

The Capulanas: These textiles are from Cape Verde, and they include striking colours and designs. Capulanas can be utilized as decorations for the home or as head wraps.

Musical Instruments: Traditional musical instruments like the "cavaquinho," a miniature guitar, and hand percussion instruments are available in Cape Verde, a country well-known for its music. These create memorable and distinctive mementos.

Local Art: Look for regional paintings, sculptures, and other creative works in art galleries and stores. Cape Verdean art frequently captures the daily life, scenery, and culture of the islands.

Grogue: You may buy bottles as mementos if you like grogue, the local spirit of Cape Verde. Numerous possibilities are available from nearby businesses and distilleries.

Local Jewelry: Select jewellery crafted from organic elements including semi-precious stones, beads, and shells. These items generally include distinctive Cape Verdean patterns.

Meals and Spices: Delectable spices and flavors from Cape Verde make wonderful mementos. Seek up "tempero crioulo," a spice and herb mixture used in Cape Verdean cuisine.

Ceramic and Pottery: Items such as plates, bowls, and ornamental pieces made of ceramic and pottery can be found produced locally. Frequently, they are made using conventional patterns and motifs.

Beachwear: Shoppers may find a wide selection of beachwear, such as bikinis, sarongs, and flip-flops, on Cape Verde's stunning beaches.

Musical CDs: Invest on CDs from regional musicians to bring the sounds of Cape Verde home. The islands, notably Cesária Évora, are renowned for their musical prowess.

Beach and Water Sports Gear: Beach and water sports equipment, including snorkelling and kitesurfing gear, is available for those who like water activities.

Local Clothing: such "panos" and "batas," may be purchased in nearby stores and marketplaces. These clothes frequently have vibrant designs on them.

Postcards and Local Art Prints: To commemorate your journey, choose up postcards and posters that showcase the breathtaking scenery and lively culture of Cape Verde.

Personalized Products: You may personalize your souvenirs and bring home a genuinely one-of-a-kind memento of your trip by ordering goods from some artists that can be customized.

To locate the ideal Cape Verdean mementos to cherish your time in this stunning and culturally diverse nation, make sure to visit the local markets, artisan festivals, and shops.

Local cuisine and dining options

African, Portuguese, and Brazilian flavours are delightfully combined in Cape Verdean food. Fresh fish, cereals, legumes, and flavorful spices are staples of the cuisine. There are several restaurants and small diners in Cape Verde that provide traditional foods, making dining there a unique gastronomic experience. Try these regional Cape Verdean foods and eating establishments:

Cachupa: Cape Verde's national food, chapau pacha, is cooked with a combination of veggies, beans and maize. Depending on the components, there are two basic varieties: Cachupa Rica (rich) and Cachupa Pobre (poor). It's often cooked with chunks of fish or pork.

Grogue: Made from sugarcane, grogue is a traditional Cape Verdean spirit. It's frequently drunk on its own or added to other recipes and drinks.

Catchupa Guisada: This stew, which is cooked with cachupa and a variety of other ingredients including meat, veggies and spices, is filling and tasty.

Lagosta à Provençal: Popular Cape Verdean seafood dish, lobster à la Provençal, is frequently served with garlic, herbs, and olive oil.

Grilled Fish: Due to Cape Verde's coastal position, fresh seafood including grouper, snapper, and tuna are abundant. One popular and delectable method of preparing seafood is grilling fish.

Xerém: Xerém is a cornmeal dish that resembles polenta. A mainstay of Cape Verdean cooking, it can be eaten with fish, pork, or beans.

Pastel de Atum: These tuna turnovers from Cape Verde are frequently offered as a snack or an appetizer. These tasty pastries have seasoned tuna inside of them.

Seafood Rice: A fragrant rice meal made with spicy herbs and spices and a variety of seafood, such as prawns, crab and mussels.

Grilled Lobster: Lobster is plentiful and delicious in Cape Verde; it's often grilled and served with butter and garlic.

Authentic Fruit: Tropical fruits including bananas, papayas, and coconuts are among the delectable produce of Cape Verde. Snack or have fresh fruit for dessert.

Cuscus: Often paired with spices, veggies, and beans, Cape Verdean couscous makes a filling side dish.

Restaurants in the Area: You may taste the genuine flavors of the islands at a number of nearby cafés and restaurants that provide traditional Cape Verdean cuisine. To experience a real Cape Verdean dinner, try eating in one of the classic "tascas".

Street Food: Offering a variety of snacks and regional delicacies like "pastéis" (pastries) and "pão com chouriço" (bread with sausage), street food vendors are prevalent across Cape Verde.

The rich history and many cultural influences of Cape Verde are reflected in the food, which is extremely superb. Enjoy the delectable and distinctive culinary traditions of the islands by sampling the regional cuisine when eating in Cape Verde.

Water Sports

A haven for lovers of the sea, the Cape Verde archipelago is situated off the coast of West Africa. Numerous aquatic sports that are both distinctive and thrilling may be found on its immaculate beaches, glistening waterways, and abundant marine life. From its well-known windsurfing sites to its undiscovered snorkelling jewels, this guide will take you deep into the world of Cape Verde's aquatic experiences.

❖ Fans of windsurfing and kitesurfing flock to Cape Verde because of its legendary trade winds. Both novices and specialists will find the perfect conditions at locations like Sal Island, particularly Santa Maria Beach. It is an unparalleled pleasure to feel the sun caress your skin and the wind blow through your sails.

❖ A rich and varied underwater ecosystem is hidden beneath the blue seas of Cape Verde. It is an ideal spot for diving and snorkelling because to the clear visibility and moderate temps. Admire a range of tropical fish species, discover vibrant coral reefs, and come across sea turtles. Unique underwater vistas may be explored in the volcanic rock formations.

❖ Deep sea fishing: Cape Verde is an ideal location for those who love to fish. Large game fish, including marlin, tuna, and dorado, abound in the deep seas that around the islands. Find the next big catch by renting a fishing boat and going on an exhilarating journey.

❖ Best sailing and yachting conditions may be found at Cape Verde. Sailing enthusiasts can find undiscovered coves and secluded beaches while circumnavigating the archipelago's many islands. An annual event that showcases the islands' rich maritime

Cape Verde Travel Guide   64

traditions, Cape Verde Ocean Week brings sailors from all over the world.

❖ Humpback whales and several dolphin species can be seen in the waters surrounding Cape Verde. To see these magnificent animals in their own environment, go on a guided boat excursion. Both nature lovers and photographers will never forget the encounter.

❖ Paddleboarding or sea kayaking around the beaches are options for a more relaxed water experience. With the freedom to explore marine caves and secret bays at your own speed, these activities provide a distinctive viewpoint on the landscapes of Cape Verde.

❖ Ten islands make up Cape Verde, and seeing them all by boat or ferry is a great way to see the archipelago. Each island has its own distinct character. From swimming in Santo Antão's natural pools to surfing on São Vicente, each island offers a varied range of aquatic activities to enjoy.

❖ Remember how wonderful it is to unwind on one of Cape Verde's breathtaking beaches. For swimming, sunbathing, or just relaxing with a good book, the warm seas and fine white dunes are alluring.

there are a variety of water sports available in Cape Verde that appeal to different kinds of travelers. This tropical haven in the Atlantic Ocean offers all one might want, be it the excitement of wind and waves or the peace of undersea exploration. You'll depart Cape Verde with lifelong memories if you plan your water experience.

Couples Activities

secret away in the Atlantic Ocean, Cape Verde is a secret treasure that presents a singular fusion of breathtaking scenery, energetic culture, and a kind, inviting vibe. Couples looking for a romantic, off-the-beaten-path retreat will find enough to choose from in this archipelago of 10 volcanic islands.

❖ The immaculate beaches of Sal Island are well known. If you're looking for a more private, calmer place to swim, consider going a bit further to Praia de Chaves. Try windsurfing or kiteboarding for an exhilarating experience, or just take a leisurely stroll hand in hand over the white beaches.

❖ Fascinating sunsets are one of Boa Vista's greatest draws. Visit the beaches in the west, such as Praia de Santa Mónica or Praia de Chaves, to witness an amazing show by night. Enjoy the peace and quiet as the sun sets on a picnic basket and a glass of locally produced Grogue.

❖ Hiking is great in the island of Santo Antão, which is characterized by rocky mountains and green valleys. Wander among terraced fields and enjoy breath-taking views as you explore the Paul Valley or the Cova Crater. For couples who love to travel, this is the ideal way to bond.

❖ Enjoy this special fusion of Portuguese and Creole cooking. Visit the restaurants in the area to sample freshly caught fish or Cachupa, a substantial stew. For a genuine taste of Cape Verdean cuisine, don't forget to try the regional wines and grog, a strong sugarcane liquor.

❖ Go to the thriving, musically and artistically rich city of Mindelo on São Vicente Island. Visit the Mercado de Peixe (Fish Market) to get a sense of local life, or see a live performance of morna, a classic Cape Verdean music genre.

❖ Diving chances in Cape Verde are exceptional. Marine life abounds in the temperate Atlantic seas. Swimming with turtles and exploring vibrant coral reefs are also options. To begin your underwater exploration, São Vicente and Sal are excellent locations.

❖ Discover several islands by taking a domestic aircraft or boat. Sal's dry surroundings and Santiago's verdant surroundings both have a distinct appeal of their own. Exploring the variety of Cape Verde through island hopping is a fascinating experience.

❖ Experience horseback riding at its best in São Nicolau. Join your significant other as you stroll around the countryside, bike on meandering trails, and soak in the peace of this little-known island.

❖ To locate distinctive Cape Verdean crafts and mementos, browse the neighbourhood markets and businesses. Gifts that are perfect mementos of your journey include handwoven baskets, elaborate ceramics, and colourful fabrics.

❖ Enjoy the splendour of the night sky in the desert on the island of Boa Vista. It's a haven for stargazers with very little light pollution. An ideal approach to cap off a romantic day is to recline and gaze at the heavens.

❖ Snorkelling is a great method to discover the marine life if you'd like an easier water sport. Take a dive into the reefs and underwater caverns to see colourful fish and maybe even a sea turtle.

❖ Whale Watching : Sperm and humpback whales often travel through the waters around Cape Verde, making it an excellent place to see whales. Experience these magnificent animals up close by going on a boat excursion.

❖ Deep Sea Fishing: A romantic outing may involve trying your hand at deep-sea fishing. Game fish like as marlin and tuna abound in the waters surrounding Cape Verde. The joy of fishing or having your catch cooked into a tasty, fresh supper are the two options available to you.

❖ Sailing: For a relaxing day on the sea, rent a catamaran or sailboat. Anchor at peaceful bays for a picnic and swim while you explore the islands' coastline. Spending quality time together is ideally achieved through this.

❖ Enjoy a beach picnic on one of Cape Verde's remote beaches for a touch of romance. Savour the regional cuisine while dining in a private setting with the soothing sound of the waves as the backdrop.

❖ Sal, specifically in Cape Verde, is renowned for its unobstructed sky. Maybe you'll see the Milky Way or some shooting stars if you spend an evening stargazing with your significant other.

Water-loving couples will find Cape Verde to be a unique location, offering a fantastic combination of adventure, romance, and natural beauty. This archipelago has fantastic things to offer any kind of couple, whether they are looking for a calm getaway on a yacht or adventure through windsurfing and kiteboarding. It's time to pack your swimwear and spirit of adventure and head to Cape Verde for an amazing trip.

Family Friendly activities

➢ Take off on a Cape Verdean excursion on Sal Island, renowned for its immaculate white sand beaches. For those who enjoy water activities like kite surfing, Santa Maria Beach is a must-see. In addition to swimming in the crystal-clear blue water, families may enjoy beachcombing and making sandcastles. For a different take, think about going fishing with a local guy or having a picnic at the beach with the family.

➢ For an introduction to Cape Verdean culture, visit São Vicente Island. See the vibrant fish market in Mindelo, where children can discover the local seafood. See traditional dancing and music at the Museu da Tabanca. Enjoy the opportunity to sample a traditional Cape Verdean supper at a nearby restaurant. To fully experience the lively rhythms of Cape Verde, your family may even enrol in a percussion workshop.

➢ A thrilling geological journey is available on Fogo Island. Take the family on a unique adventure by hiking up the Pico do Fogo volcano. Nothing compares to the bizarre lunar scenery at the top. Don't miss the opportunity to explore São Filipe, a quaint colonial town with vibrant architecture. You may sample local wine produced from grapes cultivated in the volcanic soil and observe traditional crafts being performed.

➢ Within the archipelago, Santiago Island is the biggest and provides a wealth of historical and cultural events. Visit the ancient Cidade Velha, a UNESCO World Heritage Site, when you arrive in Praia, the capital. The rich history of Cape Verde is on display in the Museu da Tabanka. Families are welcome to peruse the artwork and traditional crafts offered by merchants at the local market.

➢ Hiker's paradise is Santo Antão Island, perfect for the daring family. Hiking and exploration possibilities abound in the lush, rough environment. Take into account escorted hikes through picturesque regions like the Paul Valley or the Cova Crater. Here, you can see striking and distinctive Cape Verdean landscapes.

➢ Water fans will love Boa Vista. The family may take a trip through the remarkable Viana Desert, which is home to kilometres of breathtaking natural features including Santa Monica Beach. Take a snorkelling or scuba diving trip to explore the underwater world. Since Cape Verde is an important loggerhead turtle nesting place, your kids may also have activities with turtle watching.

➢ Peaceful Maio Island is a serene haven. Relaxing family vacations are perfect in Maio, which has calm beaches like Ponta Preta and Calheta. Additionally, you may go to the salt flats and embark on a tour to witness different bird species and flamingos. On Maio, the leisurely pace of life is ideal for spending time with loved ones.

➢ You may explore the islands' natural beauty and various cultures while making enduring experiences with your family in Cape Verde. During your stay, don't forget to show respect for the environment, the pleasant locals, and their culture. Take pleasure in your special family trip to this alluring location.

Off-the-beaten-path destinations

A unique and peaceful experience may be had by daring travelers in certain off-the-beaten-path locales, even though Cape Verde is well-known for its breathtaking beaches and well-liked tourist spots. In Cape Verde, you should think about visiting these lesser-known locations.

Saint Anthony: Despite being a bigger island in the Cape Verde chain, Santo Antão is frequently eclipsed by Sal and Boa Vista. But Santo Antão is a secret treasure for those who enjoy the outdoors and trekking because of its gorgeous scenery, hiking paths, and quaint settlements.

Fogo Island: A Visit to Fogo Island In contrast to some of the other islands, Fogo is still rarely visited despite being well-known for its active volcano. You may take in the island's distinctive wines, experience the volcanic scenery, and visit the old town of São Filipe.

São Nicolau: Rich valleys and untamed mountains are among the diverse vistas that São Nicolau has to offer. There are possibilities to explore the varied landscape, making it a great place to go hiking.

Brava Island: The smallest of the inhabited Cape Verdean islands, Brava is also known as the "Island of Flowers." Rich nature and quaint villages are its main features. It's a serene location perfect for leisure and nature enthusiasts.

Cidade Velha, Santiago: Tourists frequently ignore Cidade Velha despite it being a UNESCO World Heritage Site. With its rich history dating back to the fifteenth century, this ancient town is full with buildings from the colonial era.

Paul Valley, Santo Antão: Small farms, charming scenery, and the native way of life may be found in Paul Valley, a less frequented part of Santo Antão. Away from the tourists, it's the perfect spot to take in the island's natural splendour.

Pedra Badejo, Santiago: You may get a more genuine taste of Cape Verdean life in this seaside village that is located away from the major tourist attractions. Take in the stunning views of the seaside and the relaxed environment.

Praia Baixo, Boa Vista: Praia Baixo is a lovely, less-frequented beach; although Boa Vista is mostly renowned for its tourist establishments, there are other, more sedate areas as well. Enjoying the tranquil surroundings and unwinding is ideal.

You may discover Cape Verde's less-traveled side in these off-the-beaten-path locales, where you can take in the scenery, local culture, and peace of mind that might be more difficult to come by in more well-known areas.

Practical Information

Health And Safety Tips

Is crucial to protect your health and well-being when visiting Cape Verde. During your visit, bear the following health and safety advice in mind:

Vaccinations: Make sure you are up to date on standard Vaccinations by seeing your healthcare professional before to your trip to Cape Verde. You could require more shots, such those for typhoid and hepatitis A, depending on your particular travel itinerary.

Travel Insurance: Take into account getting comprehensive insurance for your trip, which should cover medical expenses. This might come in handy if you become sick or hurt unexpectedly.

Avoid Dehydration: It may get hot and dry in Cape Verde. Staying hydrated is important, especially if you're exercising outside or spending time in the sun.

Sun Protection: To prevent sunburn and diseases linked to the heat, wear a hat, use sunscreen, and shield your skin from the sun. There is a lot of sun in Cape Verde.

Safety of Food and Water: Take care with the food and beverages you consume. To reduce the risk of foodborne infections, stick to bottled water, steer clear of street food from unclean sellers, and select prepared and hot foods.

Prevention of Insects: Mosquitoes may be present, depending on the season and where you live. Wear long sleeves, apply bug repellent and think about booking a room with screened windows.

Local Laws and Customs: Become acquainted with the laws and customs of Cape Verde. Honor the nation's cultural customs and conventions.

Personal Belongings: Particularly in busy places and tourist destinations, keep a watch on your personal possessions. Keep valuables in hotel safes.

Petty Crime: Despite the country's relative safety, there are occasional cases of small-time thievery. In busy areas, be mindful of your possessions and handle them with caution.

Cape Verde Travel Guide

Emergency Services: Be familiar with Cape Verde's emergency phone numbers. The police emergency number is 132, while the medical emergency number is 130.

Natural Hazards: Given that Cape Verde is prone to volcanic activity, keep yourself updated on local circumstances and heed any safety advice given by authorities.

Respect the Environment: Pay attention to the fauna and surrounding surroundings. Keep your distance from wildlife, and don't trash.

Transportation Safety: When commuting between the islands by boat or plane, choose reputable carriers and adhere to safety precautions.

Health Facilities: Find the closest hospitals and medical centres in the event of an emergency. Having a little first-aid kit on you when traveling is a smart idea.

Local Suggestions: When participating in outdoor activities like hiking, be sure to check the local weather and get advice from tour operators or local authorities.

Cape Verde Travel Guide

Swimming Safety: Consider the local circumstances and adhere to safety recommendations if you intend to swim or engage in water sports. Seas off the coast of Cape Verde may be rather powerful.

You may have a fun and safe trip to Cape Verde by being aware and implementing the necessary safety measures. While visiting this stunning location, always put your health and safety first.

Language And Communication

In formal communication, education, and administration, Portuguese is the official language of Cape Verde. Speaking formally, among friends and family, and in daily life, Cape Verdeans also speak Cape Verdean Creole (Kriolu or Crioulo), a creole language based on Portuguese. The latter is frequently used for informal discussion, even though many Cape Verdeans are multilingual in both Portuguese and Cape Verdean Creole.

It might be useful to know a few simple Portuguese words even though Cape Verdean Creole is frequently spoken, particularly in everyday interactions. Many individuals can converse in

Portuguese and comprehend it, as you will discover.

When engaging in conversation with locals, remember to greet them with courtesy and respect. "Olá" (Hello), "Bom dia" (Good morning), "Boa tarde" (Good afternoon), and "Boa noite" (Good evening) are common greetings in Cape Verde.

To effectively communicate with locals, pick up a few words in Cape Verdean Creole. Simply saying hello and using basic phrases in Creole may make a more personal connection.

The significance of non-verbal communication, including hand gestures and facial expressions, is noteworthy in Cape Verdean culture. During talks, be mindful of these indications.

The culture of Cape Verde places a high importance on civility and respect. Refer to someone as "Senhor" (Mr.) or "Senhora" (Mrs.) when you speak to them, especially if they are older. In your conversations, it's critical to treat others with respect.

Never hesitate to talk to locals when you approach them. Tourists are usually received with warmth and kindness by the people of Cape Verde.

In comparison to other countries, Cape Verde has an often slower pace of life. When talking with locals, be patient and take your time.

Never take pictures of individuals without their consent, especially in remote locations. If they decline, honor their wishes.

English-speaking people can be found even in places where it is not the primary language, such as in the travel and tourism sector and hotels and eateries.

To help with communication and offer direction, tourist information centres and guides are available at popular tourist locations.

Warm hospitality is a characteristic of Cape Verdeans. You will improve your vacation experience and make lifelong memories if you make an attempt to interact with people and show respect for their culture.

Useful phrase

Here are some useful phrases in both Portuguese and Cape Verdean Creole to help you communicate during your visit to Cape Verde

Common Portuguese Phrases

- ❖ Hello - Olá
- ❖ Good morning - Bom dia
- ❖ Good afternoon - Boa tarde
- ❖ Good evening - Boa noite
- ❖ How are you? - Como está?
- ❖ Thank you - Obrigado (male) / Obrigada (female)
- ❖ Please - Por favor
- ❖ Yes - Sim
- ❖ No - Não
- ❖ Excuse me - Com licença
- ❖ I don't understand - Não entendo
- ❖ Help - Ajuda
- ❖ How much does it cost? - Quanto custa?
- ❖ Where is the bathroom? - Onde fica a casa de banho?
- ❖ I need a doctor - Preciso de um médico
- ❖ My name is [Your Name] - O meu nome é
- ❖ Can you speak English? - Fala inglês?
- ❖ I'm lost - Estou perdido

- ❖ Cheers! - Saúde!

Common Cape Verdean Creole Phrases

- ❖ Hello - Olá / Salut
- ❖ How are you? - Kusé ki bô ta bem?
- ❖ Thank you - Obrigadu (male) / Obrigada (female)
- ❖ Please - Por favor / Pufavor
- ❖ Yes - Sim
- ❖ No - Nâ
- ❖ Goodbye - Adeus / Bai
- ❖ I'm lost - N'tâ perdê
- ❖ How much does it cost? - Kusé ki valor?
- ❖ Excuse me - Dispensa
- ❖ What is your name? - Kusé ki bô nomi?
- ❖ My name is [Your Name] - Nômi d'mi
- ❖ I don't understand - N'tâ kumprênde
- ❖ Can you help me? - Bô pudi mim?
- ❖ Where is [Location]? - Undi ki fika?
- ❖ I need help - N'kreja ajuda
- ❖ Water - Agua
- ❖ Food - Mantche
- ❖ Beach - Praia
- ❖ How much is this? - Kusé ki es vende pa?

Learning a few basic phrases in both Portuguese and Cape Verdean Creole can enhance your travel experience and help you communicate with the locals in Cape Verde. It's a gesture of respect and will be appreciated by those you meet during your journey.

Local customs and etiquette

Though most people in Cape Verde are kind and pleasant, it's still a good idea to be mindful of cultural differences and follow local customs and etiquette. When traveling to Cape Verde, bear the following customs and manners in mind.

Greetings: In Cape Verde, greetings often involve a handshake. It is traditional to shake hands when you first meet someone. Using titles like "Senhor" (Mr.) or "Senhora" (Mrs.) followed by the person's last name is considered respectful when addressing someone.

Respect for Elders: The culture of Cape Verde is very focused on showing respect to elders. Be considerate and respectful to senior citizens.

Dress Modestly: Although Cape Verde is a somewhat casual location when it comes to dress codes, particularly in tourist areas, it is courteous to wear modest clothing when visiting nearby towns and religious sites.

Swimwear: is fine at the beach, but make sure you cover up while you're not in the designated area.

Public Affection: In general, Cape Verdeans are modest and discreet when it comes to showing affection in public. When showing physical affection in public, it's best to keep it inconspicuous.

Shoes: When you enter someone's home, it is traditional to take off your shoes. While paying a visit to a Cape Verdean home, always make sure this is expected.

Tonality: Though Cape Verdean Creole, or Kriolu, is commonly spoken, Portuguese is the official language. The natives would welcome you learning a few simple Creole words.

Tipping: Although it's not often required, tipping is appreciated for other services, such as good service at restaurants.

Respect Religious Practises: Since Roman Catholicism predominates in Cape Verde, many locals place a high value on religious observance.

Show consideration for religious rites and places of worship.

Involvement in the Community: Accept invitations to social gatherings and house visits as an honor, and participate in the customs and culture of the area.

Be Patient and Flexible: Cape Verdeans don't always adhere to timetables since they have a laid-back attitude towards time. Flexibility and patience are crucial.

Conservation and Respect for Nature: Cape Verde is attempting to maintain its natural environment and promote eco-tourism. By avoiding trash and adopting sustainable practices, you can demonstrate your regard for the environment.

Respect Local Customs: Be receptive to acquiring knowledge about customs and traditions in the area, and engage with dignity when asked.

People from Cape Verde are typically amiable and welcoming, and they value tourists who are interested in their customs and culture. You may make your trip to Cape Verde more fulfilling and enlightening by showing respect for and knowledge of the native ways of life.

FAREWELL

Remember that your trip to Cape Verde is only the beginning of a lifetime love affair with a place that will always hold a special place in your heart when your experience comes to an end. You've chosen more than simply knowledge by selecting this guide; you've decided to get fully immersed in the folklore, culture, and friendliness of the Cape Verdean people.

There is more to discover about Cape Verde than meets the eye; it's a journey that will change the way you see the world, make cherished memories, and broaden your viewpoint. Our goal is for your journey to Cape Verde to become a change, not merely a trip.

We express our gratitude for your selection of this guide, and we wish you happiness, exploration, and life-enriching experiences along the way. Your key to unlocking Cape Verde's full potential is here, and it's waiting for you."

Warm Regards

Printed in Great Britain
by Amazon